50 Decadent Chocolate Desserts for Home

By: Kelly Johnson

Table of Contents

- Classic Chocolate Lava Cake
- Triple Chocolate Brownies
- Chocolate Mousse
- Chocolate Ganache Tart
- Flourless Chocolate Cake
- Chocolate Soufflé
- Chocolate Cheesecake
- Molten Chocolate Bundt Cake
- Chocolate Fudge
- Chocolate Éclairs
- Chocolate Chip Cookies
- Dark Chocolate Truffles
- Chocolate Tiramisu
- Chocolate Swiss Roll
- Chocolate Meringue Pie
- Chocolate-Covered Strawberries
- Chocolate Pudding
- Double Chocolate Muffins
- Chocolate Peanut Butter Cups
- Chocolate Babka
- Hot Chocolate Affogato
- Rocky Road Fudge
- Chocolate Ice Cream
- Chocolate Croissants (Pain au Chocolat)
- S'mores Bars
- Chocolate Macarons
- Chocolate Cream Pie
- Chocolate Chip Banana Bread
- White Chocolate Raspberry Blondies
- Dark Chocolate Bark with Nuts
- Chocolate Marshmallow Squares
- Chocolate Pots de Crème
- Chocolate Bread Pudding
- Mocha Mousse Cake
- Chocolate Chia Pudding

- Chocolate Biscotti
- German Chocolate Cake
- Chocolate Tart with Sea Salt
- Nutella-Stuffed Crepes
- Chocolate Peanut Butter Fudge
- Black Forest Cake
- Chocolate Pound Cake
- Chocolate Profiteroles
- Chocolate Icebox Cake
- Dark Chocolate Panna Cotta
- Chocolate-Dipped Pretzels
- Chocolate Coconut Macaroons
- Chocolate-Covered Almonds
- White Chocolate Mousse
- Chocolate Doughnuts

Classic Chocolate Lava Cake

Ingredients:

- ½ cup (113g) unsalted butter
- 4 oz (115g) dark chocolate, chopped
- 2 eggs
- 2 egg yolks
- ¼ cup (50g) granulated sugar
- 2 tablespoons all-purpose flour
- ½ teaspoon vanilla extract
- Pinch of salt

Instructions:

1. **Preheat oven** to 425°F (220°C) and grease ramekins.
2. **Melt chocolate & butter:** Stir together until smooth.
3. **Whisk eggs & sugar:** Beat until light and thick.
4. **Combine:** Fold in melted chocolate, vanilla, salt, and flour.
5. **Bake** for 12-14 minutes until edges are firm but center is soft.

Triple Chocolate Brownies

Ingredients:

- 1 cup (226g) unsalted butter, melted
- 1 cup (200g) brown sugar
- 1 cup (200g) granulated sugar
- 3 eggs
- 1 teaspoon vanilla extract
- 1 cup (120g) cocoa powder
- 1 cup (125g) all-purpose flour
- ½ teaspoon salt
- ½ teaspoon baking powder
- ½ cup (85g) dark chocolate chips
- ½ cup (85g) white chocolate chips

Instructions:

1. **Preheat oven** to 350°F (175°C) and line a baking dish.
2. **Mix wet ingredients:** Beat butter, sugars, eggs, and vanilla.
3. **Combine dry ingredients:** Mix cocoa, flour, salt, and baking powder, then add to wet ingredients.
4. **Fold in chocolate chips.**
5. **Bake** for 25-30 minutes.

Chocolate Mousse

Ingredients:

- 6 oz (170g) dark chocolate, melted
- 3 eggs, separated
- ¼ cup (50g) granulated sugar
- ½ teaspoon vanilla extract
- 1 cup (240ml) heavy cream

Instructions:

1. **Whisk egg yolks & sugar** over low heat until thick. Stir in vanilla.
2. **Fold in melted chocolate.**
3. **Whip egg whites** until stiff peaks form.
4. **Whip heavy cream** until soft peaks form.
5. **Fold everything together** and chill for 2 hours.

Chocolate Ganache Tart

Ingredients:

- **For the Crust:**
    - 1 ½ cups (180g) crushed chocolate cookies
    - ¼ cup (60g) melted butter
- **For the Ganache Filling:**
    - 1 cup (240ml) heavy cream
    - 8 oz (225g) dark chocolate, chopped
    - 1 teaspoon vanilla extract

Instructions:

1. **Prepare crust:** Mix crushed cookies and butter, press into a tart pan, and chill.
2. **Make ganache:** Heat cream, pour over chocolate, stir until smooth, and mix in vanilla.
3. **Assemble & Chill:** Pour ganache into crust and refrigerate for 3 hours.

Flourless Chocolate Cake

Ingredients:

- 8 oz (225g) dark chocolate, melted
- ½ cup (113g) unsalted butter, melted
- ¾ cup (150g) granulated sugar
- 3 eggs
- ½ cup (60g) cocoa powder
- 1 teaspoon vanilla extract

Instructions:

1. **Preheat oven** to 350°F (175°C) and grease a cake pan.
2. **Mix wet ingredients:** Whisk chocolate, butter, sugar, eggs, and vanilla.
3. **Add cocoa powder and mix well.**
4. **Bake** for 25 minutes.

Chocolate Soufflé

Ingredients:

- 4 oz (115g) dark chocolate, melted
- 2 tablespoons unsalted butter
- 2 eggs, separated
- 2 tablespoons granulated sugar
- ½ teaspoon vanilla extract
- Pinch of salt

Instructions:

1. **Preheat oven** to 375°F (190°C) and butter ramekins.
2. **Melt chocolate & butter together.**
3. **Whisk yolks & sugar, then mix with chocolate.**
4. **Whip egg whites** until stiff, then fold into chocolate mixture.
5. **Bake** for 12-15 minutes.

Chocolate Cheesecake

Ingredients:

- **For the Crust:**
    - 1 ½ cups (180g) crushed chocolate cookies
    - ¼ cup (60g) melted butter
- **For the Filling:**
    - 12 oz (340g) cream cheese, softened
    - ¾ cup (150g) granulated sugar
    - ½ cup (120ml) heavy cream
    - 2 eggs
    - 6 oz (170g) melted dark chocolate

Instructions:

1. **Preheat oven** to 325°F (165°C).
2. **Make crust** and press into a cheesecake pan.
3. **Mix filling:** Beat cream cheese, sugar, eggs, and cream, then stir in chocolate.
4. **Bake** for 45 minutes and cool before serving.

Molten Chocolate Bundt Cake

Ingredients:

- 1 cup (226g) unsalted butter
- 1 cup (200g) brown sugar
- 4 eggs
- 1 teaspoon vanilla extract
- 1 cup (120g) cocoa powder
- 1 cup (125g) all-purpose flour
- ½ teaspoon salt
- ½ cup (120ml) hot water

Instructions:

1. **Preheat oven** to 350°F (175°C) and grease a bundt pan.
2. **Mix wet ingredients:** Beat butter, sugar, eggs, and vanilla.
3. **Combine dry ingredients:** Mix cocoa, flour, and salt, then add to wet ingredients.
4. **Add hot water & mix until smooth.**
5. **Bake** for 30 minutes.

Chocolate Fudge

Ingredients:

- 2 cups (340g) dark chocolate, chopped
- 1 can (14 oz / 400ml) sweetened condensed milk
- 1 teaspoon vanilla extract
- Pinch of salt

Instructions:

1. **Melt chocolate** with condensed milk over low heat.
2. **Stir in vanilla and salt.**
3. **Pour into a lined pan and chill** for 2 hours.

Chocolate Éclairs

Ingredients:

- **For the Choux Pastry:**
    - ½ cup (120ml) water
    - ¼ cup (56g) butter
    - ½ cup (60g) all-purpose flour
    - 2 eggs
- **For the Filling:**
    - 1 cup (240ml) heavy cream
    - ¼ cup (50g) granulated sugar
    - ½ teaspoon vanilla extract
- **For the Chocolate Glaze:**
    - ½ cup (85g) dark chocolate, melted
    - 2 tablespoons heavy cream

Instructions:

1. **Preheat oven** to 400°F (200°C).
2. **Make choux pastry:** Boil water and butter, stir in flour, then add eggs. Pipe onto a baking sheet and bake for 25 minutes.
3. **Whip cream filling** with sugar and vanilla.
4. **Fill éclairs and top with melted chocolate glaze.**

Chocolate Chip Cookies

Ingredients:

- 1 cup (226g) unsalted butter, softened
- 1 cup (200g) brown sugar
- ½ cup (100g) granulated sugar
- 2 eggs
- 1 teaspoon vanilla extract
- 2 ½ cups (315g) all-purpose flour
- 1 teaspoon baking soda
- ½ teaspoon salt
- 2 cups (340g) chocolate chips

Instructions:

1. **Preheat oven** to 350°F (175°C).
2. **Mix wet ingredients:** Beat butter, sugars, eggs, and vanilla.
3. **Combine dry ingredients:** Mix flour, baking soda, and salt, then add to wet ingredients.
4. **Fold in chocolate chips.**
5. **Bake** for 10-12 minutes.

Dark Chocolate Truffles

Ingredients:

- 8 oz (225g) dark chocolate, chopped
- ½ cup (120ml) heavy cream
- 1 teaspoon vanilla extract
- ¼ cup (30g) cocoa powder (for coating)

Instructions:

1. **Heat cream:** In a saucepan, warm heavy cream until simmering.
2. **Melt chocolate:** Pour hot cream over chocolate, let sit for 2 minutes, then stir until smooth.
3. **Chill:** Refrigerate for 1 hour until firm.
4. **Form truffles:** Scoop and roll into balls, then coat in cocoa powder.
5. **Chill again before serving.**

Chocolate Tiramisu

Ingredients:

- 8 oz (225g) mascarpone cheese
- ½ cup (100g) granulated sugar
- 1 cup (240ml) heavy cream
- 2 tablespoons cocoa powder
- 1 cup (240ml) brewed espresso
- 2 tablespoons coffee liqueur (optional)
- 20 ladyfingers
- 4 oz (115g) dark chocolate, grated

Instructions:

1. **Whip cream:** Beat heavy cream and sugar until stiff peaks form.
2. **Mix mascarpone & cocoa powder, then fold into whipped cream.**
3. **Dip ladyfingers in espresso & coffee liqueur.**
4. **Layer soaked ladyfingers, mascarpone mixture, and grated chocolate.**
5. **Chill for at least 4 hours before serving.**

Chocolate Swiss Roll

Ingredients:

- ½ cup (60g) all-purpose flour
- ¼ cup (25g) cocoa powder
- ½ teaspoon baking powder
- 4 eggs
- ½ cup (100g) granulated sugar
- 1 teaspoon vanilla extract
- 1 cup (240ml) whipped cream
- ½ cup (90g) melted chocolate (for glaze)

Instructions:

1. **Preheat oven** to 375°F (190°C) and line a baking sheet.
2. **Whisk eggs & sugar** until light and fluffy.
3. **Sift flour, cocoa, and baking powder, then fold into egg mixture.**
4. **Spread batter onto baking sheet & bake** for 10-12 minutes.
5. **Roll cake in a towel & cool, then unroll and spread whipped cream.**
6. **Roll back up, glaze with melted chocolate, and chill before serving.**

Chocolate Meringue Pie

Ingredients:

- **For the Crust:**
    - 1 ½ cups (180g) crushed graham crackers
    - ¼ cup (60g) melted butter
- **For the Filling:**
    - 2 cups (480ml) whole milk
    - ½ cup (100g) granulated sugar
    - ¼ cup (30g) cocoa powder
    - ¼ cup (30g) cornstarch
    - 3 egg yolks
    - 1 teaspoon vanilla extract
- **For the Meringue:**
    - 3 egg whites
    - ¼ cup (50g) granulated sugar

Instructions:

1. **Preheat oven** to 350°F (175°C).
2. **Prepare crust:** Mix graham crackers and butter, press into a pie pan, and bake for 10 minutes.
3. **Make filling:** Heat milk, sugar, cocoa, cornstarch, and egg yolks, whisking until thick. Stir in vanilla. Pour into crust.
4. **Make meringue:** Whip egg whites and sugar until stiff peaks form, then spread over filling.
5. **Bake** for 10 minutes until golden brown.

Chocolate-Covered Strawberries

Ingredients:

- 12 fresh strawberries
- 6 oz (170g) dark chocolate, melted
- 1 tablespoon coconut oil (optional)

Instructions:

1. **Melt chocolate** with coconut oil until smooth.
2. **Dip strawberries** into melted chocolate, letting excess drip off.
3. **Chill** on parchment paper for 20 minutes until set.

Chocolate Pudding

Ingredients:

- 2 cups (480ml) whole milk
- ½ cup (100g) granulated sugar
- ¼ cup (30g) cocoa powder
- ¼ cup (30g) cornstarch
- ¼ teaspoon salt
- ½ teaspoon vanilla extract
- 2 oz (60g) dark chocolate, chopped

Instructions:

1. **Heat milk, sugar, cocoa, cornstarch, and salt** in a saucepan, whisking until thick.
2. **Remove from heat, stir in vanilla & chocolate.**
3. **Chill** for 2 hours before serving.

Double Chocolate Muffins

Ingredients:

- 1 ¾ cups (220g) all-purpose flour
- ½ cup (50g) cocoa powder
- 1 teaspoon baking soda
- ½ teaspoon salt
- ¾ cup (150g) brown sugar
- 2 eggs
- 1 cup (240ml) buttermilk
- ½ cup (113g) unsalted butter, melted
- 1 cup (170g) chocolate chips

Instructions:

1. **Preheat oven** to 375°F (190°C) and line a muffin tin.
2. **Mix dry ingredients:** Flour, cocoa, baking soda, salt, and sugar.
3. **Mix wet ingredients:** Beat eggs, buttermilk, and melted butter.
4. **Combine & fold in chocolate chips.**
5. **Bake** for 18-20 minutes.

Chocolate Peanut Butter Cups

Ingredients:

- 1 cup (170g) dark chocolate, melted
- ½ cup (120g) peanut butter
- 2 tablespoons powdered sugar
- ½ teaspoon vanilla extract

Instructions:

1. **Fill mini muffin liners with melted chocolate** and chill.
2. **Mix peanut butter, powdered sugar, and vanilla.**
3. **Spoon peanut butter mixture into chocolate cups.**
4. **Top with more melted chocolate & chill** until set.

Chocolate Babka

Ingredients:

- **For the Dough:**
    - 2 ¾ cups (340g) all-purpose flour
    - ¼ cup (50g) sugar
    - 1 teaspoon salt
    - 1 packet (7g) yeast
    - ½ cup (120ml) warm milk
    - 2 eggs
    - ½ cup (113g) unsalted butter, softened
- **For the Filling:**
    - ½ cup (115g) butter, melted
    - ½ cup (100g) brown sugar
    - 1 cup (170g) dark chocolate, chopped

Instructions:

1. **Make dough:** Mix flour, sugar, salt, yeast, milk, and eggs. Knead in butter. Let rise for 1 hour.
2. **Roll out dough, spread melted butter, sugar, and chocolate.**
3. **Roll into a log, slice lengthwise, twist, and place in loaf pan.**
4. **Let rise for 30 minutes, then bake** at 350°F (175°C) for 35-40 minutes.

Hot Chocolate Affogato

Ingredients:

- 1 cup (240ml) hot chocolate
- 2 scoops vanilla ice cream
- ½ oz (15g) dark chocolate, grated

Instructions:

1. **Make hot chocolate.**
2. **Place ice cream in a cup.**
3. **Pour hot chocolate over ice cream.**
4. **Sprinkle with grated chocolate & serve immediately.**

Rocky Road Fudge

Ingredients:

- 2 cups (340g) dark chocolate, chopped
- 1 can (14 oz / 400ml) sweetened condensed milk
- 1 teaspoon vanilla extract
- 1 cup (100g) mini marshmallows
- ½ cup (60g) chopped almonds or walnuts

Instructions:

1. **Melt chocolate and condensed milk** together over low heat.
2. **Stir in vanilla, marshmallows, and nuts.**
3. **Pour into a lined pan and chill** for 2 hours before cutting.

Chocolate Ice Cream

Ingredients:

- 2 cups (480ml) heavy cream
- 1 cup (240ml) whole milk
- ¾ cup (150g) granulated sugar
- ½ cup (50g) cocoa powder
- 4 egg yolks
- 1 teaspoon vanilla extract
- 4 oz (115g) dark chocolate, melted

Instructions:

1. **Heat milk, cream, cocoa, and sugar** until warm.
2. **Whisk egg yolks**, then slowly add warm mixture.
3. **Cook over low heat** until thick, then stir in melted chocolate and vanilla.
4. **Chill, then churn** in an ice cream maker.

Chocolate Croissants (Pain au Chocolat)

Ingredients:

- 1 sheet puff pastry, thawed
- 4 oz (115g) dark chocolate, chopped
- 1 egg, beaten (for egg wash)

Instructions:

1. **Preheat oven** to 375°F (190°C).
2. **Cut pastry into rectangles, place chocolate in center, and roll up.**
3. **Brush with egg wash and bake** for 15-18 minutes.

S'mores Bars

Ingredients:

- 1 ½ cups (180g) graham cracker crumbs
- ½ cup (113g) melted butter
- 1 cup (170g) chocolate chips
- 1 cup (100g) mini marshmallows
- ½ cup (120ml) sweetened condensed milk

Instructions:

1. **Preheat oven** to 350°F (175°C).
2. **Mix crumbs & butter**, press into a baking dish.
3. **Layer chocolate, marshmallows, and condensed milk.**
4. **Bake** for 20 minutes.

Chocolate Macarons

Ingredients:

- 1 cup (100g) almond flour
- 1 cup (125g) powdered sugar
- ¼ cup (25g) cocoa powder
- 2 egg whites
- ¼ cup (50g) granulated sugar

For the Filling:

- 4 oz (115g) dark chocolate, melted
- ¼ cup (60ml) heavy cream

Instructions:

1. **Sift almond flour, powdered sugar, and cocoa.**
2. **Whip egg whites & sugar** to stiff peaks, then fold in dry ingredients.
3. **Pipe onto a baking sheet, let rest 30 minutes.**
4. **Bake** at 300°F (150°C) for 15 minutes.
5. **Make ganache & sandwich between cookies.**

Chocolate Cream Pie

Ingredients:

- 1 pre-baked pie crust
- 2 cups (480ml) whole milk
- ½ cup (100g) sugar
- ¼ cup (30g) cocoa powder
- ¼ cup (30g) cornstarch
- 3 egg yolks
- 1 teaspoon vanilla extract
- 4 oz (115g) dark chocolate, chopped

Instructions:

1. **Heat milk, sugar, cocoa, cornstarch, and yolks**, whisking until thick.
2. **Stir in chocolate & vanilla.**
3. **Pour into pie crust & chill** for 3 hours.

Chocolate Chip Banana Bread

Ingredients:

- 2 ripe bananas, mashed
- ½ cup (113g) butter, melted
- ¾ cup (150g) brown sugar
- 2 eggs
- 1 teaspoon vanilla extract
- 1 ½ cups (190g) all-purpose flour
- 1 teaspoon baking soda
- ½ teaspoon salt
- ½ cup (85g) chocolate chips

Instructions:

1. **Preheat oven** to 350°F (175°C).
2. **Mix wet ingredients:** Bananas, butter, sugar, eggs, vanilla.
3. **Combine dry ingredients:** Flour, baking soda, salt, then mix into wet.
4. **Fold in chocolate chips & bake** for 50 minutes.

White Chocolate Raspberry Blondies

Ingredients:

- ½ cup (113g) unsalted butter, melted
- ¾ cup (150g) brown sugar
- 1 egg
- 1 teaspoon vanilla extract
- 1 cup (125g) all-purpose flour
- ½ teaspoon baking powder
- ½ cup (85g) white chocolate chips
- ½ cup (75g) fresh raspberries

Instructions:

1. **Preheat oven** to 350°F (175°C).
2. **Mix wet ingredients:** Butter, sugar, egg, vanilla.
3. **Combine dry ingredients:** Flour, baking powder, then mix into wet.
4. **Fold in white chocolate & raspberries.**
5. **Bake** for 25 minutes.

Dark Chocolate Bark with Nuts

Ingredients:

- 12 oz (340g) dark chocolate, melted
- ½ cup (60g) almonds, chopped
- ½ cup (60g) pistachios, chopped
- ¼ teaspoon sea salt

Instructions:

1. **Melt chocolate** and spread onto parchment paper.
2. **Sprinkle nuts & sea salt.**
3. **Chill for 1 hour, then break into pieces.**

Chocolate Marshmallow Squares

Ingredients:

- 2 cups (340g) dark chocolate, melted
- 1 cup (100g) mini marshmallows
- ½ cup (120g) peanut butter

Instructions:

1. **Melt chocolate & peanut butter.**
2. **Stir in marshmallows.**
3. **Spread in a lined pan & chill** for 2 hours.

Chocolate Pots de Crème

Ingredients:

- 6 oz (170g) dark chocolate, chopped
- 1 cup (240ml) heavy cream
- ½ cup (120ml) whole milk
- 3 egg yolks
- ¼ cup (50g) granulated sugar
- 1 teaspoon vanilla extract

Instructions:

1. **Heat cream & milk** until warm.
2. **Whisk yolks & sugar**, then slowly add warm mixture.
3. **Stir in chocolate & vanilla.**
4. **Bake in ramekins at 325°F (160°C) in a water bath for 30 minutes.**
5. **Chill before serving.**

Chocolate Bread Pudding

Ingredients:

- 4 cups (200g) cubed bread (brioche or challah)
- 2 cups (480ml) whole milk
- ½ cup (120ml) heavy cream
- ½ cup (100g) granulated sugar
- ½ cup (85g) dark chocolate, chopped
- 2 eggs
- 1 teaspoon vanilla extract
- ½ teaspoon cinnamon

Instructions:

1. **Preheat oven** to 350°F (175°C) and grease a baking dish.
2. **Heat milk, cream, sugar, and chocolate** until melted.
3. **Whisk eggs & vanilla**, then mix with chocolate mixture.
4. **Soak bread cubes** in mixture for 15 minutes.
5. **Bake** for 35-40 minutes.

Mocha Mousse Cake

Ingredients:

- **For the Cake:**
    - 1 ½ cups (190g) all-purpose flour
    - ½ cup (50g) cocoa powder
    - 1 teaspoon baking powder
    - ½ teaspoon salt
    - 1 cup (200g) sugar
    - ½ cup (120ml) strong coffee
    - ½ cup (120ml) milk
    - ½ cup (113g) melted butter
    - 2 eggs
- **For the Mousse:**
    - 1 cup (240ml) heavy cream
    - 6 oz (170g) dark chocolate, melted
    - 2 tablespoons espresso powder

Instructions:

1. **Preheat oven** to 350°F (175°C).
2. **Make cake batter:** Mix dry and wet ingredients separately, then combine.
3. **Bake** for 25-30 minutes.
4. **Make mousse:** Whip cream, fold in melted chocolate and espresso powder.
5. **Layer mousse over cake & chill** for 2 hours.

Chocolate Chia Pudding

Ingredients:

- 2 cups (480ml) almond milk
- ½ cup (90g) chia seeds
- ¼ cup (25g) cocoa powder
- ¼ cup (60ml) maple syrup
- 1 teaspoon vanilla extract

Instructions:

1. **Whisk all ingredients together.**
2. **Refrigerate for at least 4 hours** or overnight.

Chocolate Biscotti

Ingredients:

- 2 cups (250g) all-purpose flour
- ½ cup (100g) granulated sugar
- ¼ cup (25g) cocoa powder
- 1 teaspoon baking powder
- ½ teaspoon salt
- 2 eggs
- ½ cup (85g) chocolate chips

Instructions:

1. **Preheat oven** to 350°F (175°C).
2. **Mix dry & wet ingredients separately, then combine.**
3. **Shape into a log, bake for 25 minutes.**
4. **Slice and bake again for 10 minutes.**

German Chocolate Cake

Ingredients:

- **For the Cake:**
    - 1 ¾ cups (220g) all-purpose flour
    - ½ cup (50g) cocoa powder
    - 1 teaspoon baking soda
    - ½ teaspoon salt
    - 1 cup (200g) sugar
    - ½ cup (120ml) buttermilk
    - ½ cup (120ml) vegetable oil
    - 2 eggs
- **For the Coconut-Pecan Frosting:**
    - 1 cup (240ml) evaporated milk
    - ½ cup (100g) brown sugar
    - ½ cup (113g) butter
    - 3 egg yolks
    - 1 cup (80g) shredded coconut
    - 1 cup (120g) chopped pecans

Instructions:

1. **Make cake batter** and bake at 350°F (175°C) for 30 minutes.
2. **Make frosting:** Cook evaporated milk, sugar, butter, and yolks until thick, then add coconut & pecans.
3. **Layer frosting between cakes.**

Chocolate Tart with Sea Salt

Ingredients:

- **For the Crust:**
    - 1 ½ cups (180g) crushed chocolate cookies
    - ¼ cup (60g) melted butter
- **For the Ganache Filling:**
    - 1 cup (240ml) heavy cream
    - 8 oz (225g) dark chocolate, chopped
    - 1 teaspoon vanilla extract
    - ½ teaspoon sea salt

Instructions:

1. **Make crust & chill.**
2. **Make ganache** by heating cream, then mixing with chocolate.
3. **Pour into crust & sprinkle with sea salt.**
4. **Chill for 3 hours before serving.**

Nutella-Stuffed Crepes

Ingredients:

- 1 cup (125g) all-purpose flour
- 1 cup (240ml) milk
- 2 eggs
- 1 tablespoon sugar
- ½ teaspoon vanilla extract
- ½ cup (120g) Nutella

Instructions:

1. **Make crepe batter & rest for 30 minutes.**
2. **Cook crepes on a skillet, flipping after 1 minute.**
3. **Spread Nutella, fold, and serve.**

Chocolate Peanut Butter Fudge

Ingredients:

- 1 cup (170g) dark chocolate, melted
- ½ cup (120g) peanut butter
- 1 can (14 oz / 400ml) sweetened condensed milk

Instructions:

1. **Melt chocolate & peanut butter together.**
2. **Stir in condensed milk.**
3. **Pour into a lined pan & chill.**

Black Forest Cake

Ingredients:

- **For the Cake:**
    - 1 ¾ cups (220g) all-purpose flour
    - ½ cup (50g) cocoa powder
    - 1 teaspoon baking soda
    - ½ teaspoon salt
    - 1 cup (200g) sugar
    - ½ cup (120ml) buttermilk
    - ½ cup (120ml) vegetable oil
    - 2 eggs
- **For the Filling:**
    - 1 cup (200g) cherry pie filling
    - 1 cup (240ml) whipped cream

Instructions:

1. **Bake cake at 350°F (175°C) for 30 minutes.**
2. **Layer whipped cream & cherry filling between cakes.**

Chocolate Pound Cake

Ingredients:

- 1 cup (226g) unsalted butter, softened
- 1 ¾ cups (220g) all-purpose flour
- ½ cup (50g) cocoa powder
- 1 teaspoon baking powder
- ½ teaspoon salt
- 1 cup (200g) sugar
- ½ cup (120ml) milk
- 4 eggs

Instructions:

1. **Preheat oven** to 350°F (175°C).
2. **Mix wet ingredients, then add dry ingredients.**
3. **Bake for 50-55 minutes.**

Chocolate Profiteroles

Ingredients:

- **For the Choux Pastry:**
    - ½ cup (120ml) water
    - ¼ cup (56g) butter
    - ½ cup (60g) all-purpose flour
    - 2 eggs
- **For the Filling:**
    - 1 cup (240ml) heavy cream
    - ¼ cup (50g) sugar
- **For the Chocolate Sauce:**
    - ½ cup (85g) dark chocolate, melted

Instructions:

1. **Make choux pastry:** Boil water & butter, stir in flour, then add eggs.
2. **Bake at 400°F (200°C) for 25 minutes.**
3. **Whip cream for filling.**
4. **Slice profiteroles, fill with cream, drizzle chocolate sauce.**

Chocolate Icebox Cake

Ingredients:

- 2 cups heavy cream
- 1/4 cup powdered sugar
- 1 tsp vanilla extract
- 1 box chocolate wafers
- 4 oz dark chocolate, shaved

Instructions:

1. Whip cream with sugar and vanilla until stiff peaks form.
2. Spread a thin layer of cream on a platter. Layer chocolate wafers and whipped cream, repeating until all are used.
3. Cover and refrigerate overnight.
4. Garnish with chocolate shavings before serving.

Dark Chocolate Panna Cotta

Ingredients:

- 2 cups heavy cream
- 1/2 cup whole milk
- 1/2 cup dark chocolate, chopped
- 1/4 cup sugar
- 1 tsp vanilla extract
- 1 1/2 tsp gelatin
- 2 tbsp cold water

Instructions:

1. Sprinkle gelatin over cold water and let sit for 5 minutes.
2. Heat cream, milk, sugar, and chocolate until melted. Stir in vanilla.
3. Remove from heat, add gelatin, and stir until dissolved.
4. Pour into molds and chill for at least 4 hours before serving.

Chocolate-Dipped Pretzels

Ingredients:

- 12 pretzel rods
- 6 oz dark chocolate, melted
- 6 oz white chocolate, melted
- Sprinkles or crushed nuts (optional)

Instructions:

1. Dip pretzels halfway into melted chocolate.
2. Lay on parchment paper and sprinkle with toppings.
3. Let set until firm before serving.

Chocolate Coconut Macaroons

Ingredients:

- 2 1/2 cups shredded coconut
- 2/3 cup sweetened condensed milk
- 1 tsp vanilla extract
- 2 egg whites
- 1/4 tsp salt
- 6 oz dark chocolate, melted

Instructions:

1. Preheat oven to 325°F (163°C). Line a baking sheet with parchment paper.
2. Mix coconut, condensed milk, and vanilla.
3. Beat egg whites with salt until stiff peaks form, then fold into the coconut mixture.
4. Drop spoonfuls onto the baking sheet and bake for 20–25 minutes.
5. Dip cooled macaroons in melted chocolate and let set.

Chocolate-Covered Almonds

Ingredients:

- 1 cup almonds
- 6 oz dark chocolate, melted
- 1/4 tsp sea salt

Instructions:

1. Toast almonds in a dry pan over medium heat for 5 minutes.
2. Coat almonds in melted chocolate, then spread on parchment paper.
3. Sprinkle with sea salt and let set before serving.

White Chocolate Mousse

Ingredients:

- 6 oz white chocolate, chopped
- 1 cup heavy cream
- 1/2 tsp vanilla extract
- 1 egg white
- 1 tbsp sugar

Instructions:

1. Melt white chocolate and let cool slightly.
2. Whip heavy cream with vanilla until soft peaks form.
3. Beat egg white with sugar until stiff peaks form, then fold into the whipped cream.
4. Gently fold in melted chocolate. Chill for at least 2 hours before serving.

Chocolate Doughnuts

Ingredients:

- 1 1/2 cups all-purpose flour
- 1/2 cup cocoa powder
- 1/2 cup sugar
- 1 tsp baking powder
- 1/2 tsp baking soda
- 1/4 tsp salt
- 1/2 cup buttermilk
- 2 eggs
- 1/4 cup melted butter
- 1 tsp vanilla extract
- 4 oz dark chocolate, melted (for glaze)

Instructions:

1. Preheat oven to 350°F (175°C). Grease a doughnut pan.
2. In a bowl, whisk flour, cocoa, sugar, baking powder, baking soda, and salt.
3. In another bowl, mix buttermilk, eggs, butter, and vanilla.
4. Combine wet and dry ingredients, then pipe into the doughnut pan.
5. Bake for 10–12 minutes. Cool and dip in melted chocolate before serving.

www.ingramcontent.com/pod-product-compliance
Lightning Source LLC
LaVergne TN
LVHW081335060526
838201LV00055B/2658